Stay Kind

♡

Madeleine Gasperi

Bullied: From Victim to Victorious

Madeleine Gasperi

To my younger self.
To the girl who
hates her body.
To the boy struggling
with his sexuality.
To the kid who sits alone
it's going to be okay.

Table of Contents

An

Introduction

Welcome to the first day of the rest of your life! Not quite, but hello to whoever is reading this. Thanks for buying a copy. You clearly have great taste in books☺ On a more serious note you are probably reading this because you are being bullied...

First of all, I am very sorry that you have to experience bullying; no one should have to. I may not be going through the exact pain you endure every day or maybe I am. I don't know exactly what you're going through. I know how you feel. I empathize with you completely. I know how much it hurts to sit alone at lunch, or what it's like to hear rumors traveling through the school.

I can empathize with how hard it is to wake up and face the day.
Some days it would be much easier just to sleep in and call in sick.

Been there, done that. I have cried my tears, and threw my pity parties. I made a conscious decision to work to make things better. *SPOILER* It all gets better. You have choices and options on whether or not it gets better.

I am writing this book to help kids like me who felt so alone, and helpless. If I knew half of the things I know now, my experiences with bullying would be different. I would have had the crap beaten out of me every day and still would have sat alone. The words said to me would be degrading and vicious, but how it affected me emotionally would have been very different.

This book is very personal to me. I do not think I'll regret what's inside, but this is me being vulnerable to help you out.

To be frank, I would regret not putting my story out there for everyone to see. My story is unique and different. My story is my story, but there is a million just like mine. To keep this really honest and authentic, I have included diary entries, my tips, and my story. My pain and anguish. But most importantly, I included the positive because...

I survived, and eventually I thrived.

If I can make it through this grim time; I know YOU CAN! It's all about how you handle it.

You can either be a Victim or you can be Victorious.

Welcome to your second chance. It's time to fight for a new beginning and earn that happy ending!

So without further ado, welcome to a journey of vulnerability, triumph, self-love, and acceptance!

Prologue

I remember the first time I felt left out. The first time, where I didn't fit in. But most importantly, I remember the very first time that I was put down. I was in the 2ND grade. This girl who was originally a ~~good~~ best friend of mine told me I was "Fat and stupid." I went home and cried that day and most likely, I probably ate. I am an emotional eater.

I remember not being included and not feeling good about myself until the 4th grade. I had toxic friends, even in elementary school. I went almost two years dressing in oversized clothes and over eating. I just felt bad. I finished off 5th grade with zero friends. People started to clique up for middle school. Here comes middle school. I moved into a different area so I start fresh at the other middle school and I only last two days.

I was excluded and transferred to the middle school where my old classmates went. Middle School was absolute hell; I was physically and emotionally beaten down. Pushed down in the locker room, you know... usual middle school stuff. I was bullied for the boys I liked, for the friends I made, and being myself. I was asked about my boobs. "You're retarded, you're gay..." Hate speech and name calling... Ladies and gentlemen, I present public school. Then of course you have your PE teachers who are just so mean. That one who probably wanted to be a pro ball player, now he blows a whistle calling out kids and calling them fat. That PE Teacher

The summer going into the 9th grade, I finally found someone I could relate to. This girl would end up being my best friend for a solid two years.

In the 9th grade, I wasn't bullied by the students I was bullied and

discriminated against by a teacher.
'That book is for gays' her words, not mine...

10th grade goes down in the books where I found my niche. A place where I belonged, that was 4th period leadership.
This was the place where I found friends who accepted me, and loved me. For once in my life I felt special!

Unfortunately, all good things come to an end. Seniors graduate. 11th grade is where everything turned upside down. I lost my best friend. The one class where I first found my group of friends is where I sat alone, and got sick physically and emotionally. This was the year where I was broken and shattered.

Now here I am summer, going into 12th grade. Ready to go pick up the pieces and start fresh. Beyond ready to leave high school, and go to college. Most importantly ready to put pen to paper open up and share my story.

An Open Letter:

This book wouldn't be possible without those who hurt me, those who didn't stick up for me and everyone else who made me feel less than.

Dear Classmates, teachers, administration, bullies, and everyone else in between.

This is not my big fat middle finger to you, where I list everyone's names... That is tacky. This is genuine thanks for a big fat juicy story!

I would first like to thank my classmates; you know who you are. Thank you for feeding into the drama that went on in that classroom. Thank you oh so very much for letting me sit alone every day. I loved having the extra seat for my purse. I really appreciate not being included in classroom conversation, I got to do a lot of thinking on my own. I had so many ideas that I kept to myself. I also got a ton of my math homework done. Thank you so much for spreading rumors about my sexuality, it made it really hard to find a boyfriend. Sure, I didn't have anyone to go out with but I sure had a lot of 'me' time. The gossip did wonders for my reputation, and how people perceived me. Thank you so much for the genuine hate that came straight from your hearts. I was really wanting to gain weight, and lose clumps of my hair at a time. Most importantly, I would like to thank everyone in that classroom for lying to the principal about me not being bullied.

That went over great. Thank you for making me feel so unsafe and sad. Pushing me to my limit was great. Leaving that class was the best thing that I could have done for my health. To each and every one of you who saw me struggling, and did nothing to help all I can say is you guys are a bunch of go-getters!

Now we can't forget the teachers and administration who made this all possible. Teachers thanks for not having a handle on the classroom. Thank you for not taking the time to make sure I was happy. Thank you for not making the kids include me in group projects. Thank you teacher. Thank you for letting me work tremendously hard on blood drives and other projects just to get donations. I really wouldn't want to forget the eye rolls I got every day and especially during my presentations or when I had a GREAT idea. It really made me realize that I will never roll my eyes again. I appreciate the most leaving the classroom, and never getting an apology from the students.

To the people who run this school; thank you for attacking me and saying I was the problem when I came to you lovely people for help. I am now more cautious about who I turn to. Thank you for role playing with that student after he cyber bullied me, rather than a proper suspension. Thank you for treating me differently because I am not an athlete. The deterioration of my health would not have been possible without the leadership of your team. But hey, all of that crying and puking burns calories! I am a stronger person. For that, I thank you! Thanks for the story... You know how much I love to write.

With my most sincere gratitude,

Madeleine Gasperi

Chapter 1: Bullying Basics

It probably is no secret that bullying isn't an issue that affects few. This social issue affects millions and millions of people all over the world. Point blank, no one is going through bullying alone. But what does bullying exactly look like? Sure, it has been portrayed in television and movies and you read the definition in a pamphlet in the school counselor's office. But what does it look like?

The truth is that it can be a very different situation for me than it can be for you. Bullying comes in so many forms.

It's physical, emotional, and due to modern technology even cyber. Bullying is more than just getting your lunch money taken, or being shoved into a locker.

My Definition of Bullying:

"Bullying is any form of harassment. Whether that be physical or emotional. Bullies often pick you apart. Truly anyone who makes you feel less than is bullying you; harming someone purposefully when they are in a vulnerable position.

The Types of Bullies

Through my own experiences with bullying, I have learned that there are many types of bullies. There is probably more, but lucky for me, I haven't had to experience any more than I did.

The Avatar: This is the person who says whatever they please from behind a computer screen.

The Big Cheese: This is the person who bullies to feel powerful or better about themselves. Tearing others down makes this person feelgood.

The Frenemy: The friend of yours who fits into any category listed. The friend who makes you feel like absolute crap.

The Gossip Columnists: The people who talk about someone behind their back in a negative way. Often the gossip material is false. Stems from boredom.

Let's Get Physical: The bully who wants to hurt you physically rather than emotionally/mentally, "I can kick you square in the jaw, but I don't know what to say."

The Parrot: This bully feels it is necessary to join in because they hear others attacking the person being bullied.

The Picker: This bully picks apart your physical appearance.

*HINT (they are only picking apart the physical appearance because they can't find anything to bash someone about)

The Self-Bully: This person is always bullying himself or herself.

There may be a large variety of bullies. But why do people bully. Why do bullies bully? Kids always think the reason they are being bullied has to do with them. Let me tell you something; it has nothing to do with you. I wish I figured this out sooner.

I always thought I was the reason people picked on me and hurt me. I thought it was my fault. It had to be me. I was doing something wrong to make people dislike me. I tried so hard to be liked and to fit in. In the later years of elementary school, I wanted to be invisible. I dressed in oversized clothes. I thought the reason was because I was going through a tomboy phase, but now it all makes sense... I was depressed. In 6th grade, I worked so hard at fitting in, even though I didn't. I didn't tell my friends about the boys I liked because they weren't the 'hot boys'. There were days I didn't pull my lunch out of the lunch box because I was just so insecure with myself.

I didn't wear my hair a certain way because I was afraid of being judged. I lied about what I watched on TV. I tried so hard to not be myself. I lost track of who I was. The more I pretended to be someone else, the more I didn't fit in. It didn't matter how hard I tried I was still a target.

So the question is if I don't have control and it isn't my fault why do people bully?

The Top Reasons People Bully

To Fit in

To hide their fears

They are internally struggling

Jealousy

To keep from getting bullied

Unhappy in their own life

Of course, there are many other reasons and as targets of bullying, all we can do is know our worth and have empathy for these bullies. We just need to wish them well and hope that they find happiness. I hope the bullies can overcome what makes them so insecure.

The bottom line is; that the reason you or someone you know is being bullied is not your fault. Bullies have deep seeded issues that make them lash out and cause others pain. Maybe the bully is unhappy in their own life and in order to feel good the gratification of putting someone down builds them up. The reason could be that they are hurting inside and are struggling.
Bullying isn't okay. It's a vicious cycle that affects millions of people each and every day.

Bottom Line: It's not your fault. Have Empathy!
❤

Chapter 2: In The Feels

If I had a dollar for every movie and TV show that inaccurately portrayed bullying; I would have a shit ton of money. Sure, there are some great stories showcased on the silver screen. (I'd list them if I had the rights) However, the movies really miss the point. In many works the films poke fun at bullying. Or the outcast is the one who is getting fun poked at them; like it's their fault. The guys get aggressive and physical, and the girls spread rumors about each other. This happens to an extent, but there are many guys who gossip and there are plenty of girls who get into fist fights.

It's much more than the 'nerd' getting shoved in a locker or the football player taking the lunch money. Why isn't the aftermath shown? Bullying is so much more than that. It takes a toll on everyone involved the family, the friends. The victim. It affects people emotionally, physically, even mentally.

It brings up the emotions of sadness, and Betrayal and embarrassment. It feels terrible, and hurts so severely. You just don't know what to do. It affects some people more than others.
There will be certain days where it doesn't bother you. There will be days where you want to lock yourself in your room, turn on sad music, and cry! I've been on both ends of the spectrum. I had a playlist of music just for those days.
#SadMusicGivesMeComfort

What Bullying Feels Like In My Eyes

- Bad menstrual cramps that no amount of pain relief can alleviate.
- Flunking your midterm.
- Getting called on in class when you don't know the answer.
- Flunking your driver's test on your birthday.
- Getting robbed.
- Plugging the toilet at someone else's house.
- Putting dry contacts in your eyes.
- Coming in last place in your sports event.
- Finding out that your best friend is moving far away.
- Getting hit by a car.
- Your parents divorcing.
- Having Strep Throat.
- Sitting on your curling iron; while it's on.
- Being constipated.
- Getting picked last.

- Wearing jeans that are way too tight.
- Getting into a car accident.
- Migraine headaches.
- Nicking yourself with a razor.
- Runner's cramps.
- Getting a bad haircut.
- Walking around with your dress tucked in your underwear all day.
- Being stung by 500 bees.
- Spinal Tap.
- Not having a partner during a project.
- Drinking Sour Milk.
- Stepping on glass.
- Getting your braces tightened.

Quite frankly, I would rather step on glass, and sit on my curling iron every day if it meant I wouldn't be isolated, and verbally attacked.

Chapter 3: My Bullying Story

I wish that I could say my junior year was a work of fiction. Unfortunately, I cannot be that lucky. This is the raw truth of what happened during the 11th grade. For the sake of privacy, I will be using symbols and other names in place of the originals.

I had an amazing summer. In fact, it could have been the perfect summer. With the perfect friends. My parents left for a few days for a sailing trip and let my best friend... Let's call her 'Sue', stay over. You know those friends you can do anything with and still feel like you conquered the world? Sue was that friend! We would just go for drives and feel like it was the best time ever! Our friendship grew and it was clear we got so much closer. We did everything together. We had painted our nails and watched movies.

We worked out and would have long talks. Where we would open up. I truly was happy. We ended that summer celebrating our two year friendship anniversary with a homemade 2 hour slide show with all our pictures. We were

#FriendshipGoals ♥

We were best friends at leadership training for the freshman-mentoring program. Then, once school started, everything changed. My best friend and I were in leadership class together. I instantly clicked with all of the students except for one. Let's call her K. K was one of Sue's good friends, but they lost touch. K never liked me... don't have a clue why not... Anyways the teacher was new to the school and this was her first time teaching leadership. Let's call this teacher Betty. I met her once over the summer. I was excited for this year because leadership was my safe space. I started making posters and really fitting in.

Things became spotty for my best friend and me. We weren't speaking nearly as much. It was cordial; not friendly on her side of the conversation.

Saturday, September 20th I received a text from her saying how I spread rumors about her. Keep in mind I only had two classes, and the people she was reporting these rumors were from people she saw during the day. Not anyone that I associate myself with. That's not being snobby, but keeping myself safe.

This friend I had kept around and cared so much about. She was no longer an acquaintance. I was so confused. The person I cared about most besides my family didn't give a shit about me. Long story short, that class got awkward and I ended up going to the counselor's office and dropping 4th period leadership class. It was so weird the one class where I found my niche and that made me so happy and safe was the place that I gave up going to because no one sat next to me or even spoke to me and I wasn't included in the slightest. Quite honestly, I think people would rather watch paint dry than talk to me. I was so puzzled and hurt. This was the class that made me feel complete. The class that once gave me a purpose and a sense of belonging was now the place I dreaded going. I would have much rather gone to Algebra 2 or even PE.

Dear Diary,

I have lost the most important friend I have ever had. I mean she's not dead but our friendship is. ▆▆▆ and I are no longer friends and its the worst feeling in the world knowing someone you used to care about more then anything could give a shit about you. We have had fights but it just isn't going to work! I have nothing more to say I am crying to hard to see

October soon approached and I was lonely. I started volunteering in the special education classroom to kill time and fill the void. While all of my old classmates were doing team building and ice breakers.

I was eating lunch with my mom and doing T.A. work. Rumors started going around the school about me and the rumors did not make any sense. I was a lesbian, then I was pregnant. I was even sleeping with Betty my leadership teacher... I was a moving target. I decided "Madeleine you are going to have so many regrets letting people choose who you are going to be and what you are going to do." *bad idea*

I had my mom call the counselor on her lunch break and had me enrolled again in the class. I joined the following day. I still didn't have any friends, and no one sat next to me. My name came up in conversation. I was always picked last. I was pushed aside. I cleaned paint brushes alone in the back… fun times nothing was getting better. I was getting depressed. I ate lunch in my favorite teacher's classroom every single day. I was lonely and alone. I went into the leadership room one day before school and spoke to my teacher, Betty. I walked in and explained to her why I left the class in the first place. When I first left I told her it was conflicting with my college workload I made it clear that it was because of the bullying I went through every damn day in her classroom. Not my workload. I was thriving in college!

She said something along the lines of "it's been awkward in here and I do sense the tension. I just don't know how to go about it." I told her I understood. During 6th period she stopped by the special education room and said. "With your permission can I pull you and her out of class tomorrow so you guys can talk?" I agreed.

The following day I walked out over to
the leadership room and sat in a chair.
Betty turned on calming music and
Sue walked in with a friend from PE. PE
was on north campus, they made the trip.
It was a ten-minute walk.

Sue immediately turned around and said "I feel
attacked, this was a setup and I'm not ready to
talk to her." She quickly left the room and
headed back down the hallway. Less than a few
minutes later, Sue returned to the classroom. She
came and sat down. Betty sat on a stool in front
of the class. She started directing us on how to
start this heart to heart. All Sue would say is
"Madeleine knows what she did."
   I still have no clue

I asked her to elaborate and explain. She said "I heard from a friend that you have been spreading secrets about me. I know it was you because they are things I only told you."

I told her "I was sorry, there are rumors going around about you, but I didn't say anything. There are tons of rumors going around about me too."
"I am so broken hearted about our friendship ending. I have tried to reach out, but I am just sick over this. It feels like a break-up." I reached out as far as I could. I tried writing four page letters, and DVDS with our pictures set to our favorite song. Nothing worked

"I am straight." She quickly replied

"I said nothing about your sexuality. I just said it hurt like a break-up. I mean Sue, we were that close. I care about you."
That was the conversation except it had a lot more crying and a lot of back and forth arguing. I did discover one reason Sue

was so hurt was because there were rumors about us being a couple. It was true, before our falling out we were practically joined at the hip. We were always together. We went to the first football game of the year and at the tailgater one of our classmates said: "You two are like never apart. I honestly never have seen you guys apart." It really all is making sense. She was so pissed off at the football game and was worried about sitting next to me. #SelfReflection.

Diary Entry 2: 11/1/14 — "The Talk"

Dear Diary,

Yesterday ███████ and I had to talk with each other. ███████, called her out of Class 6th period and made us have a heart to heart. I have come to the conclusion that a large part of our thing was there was speculation we were a couple. I never thought of us more than friends. I don't need her. We have made progress, but we are no where near friends. ███████ sees right through her. It's fake. I am truly disgusted are friendship ended because she thought I had feelings for her. My mom also thought I liked ███████. I am going to be okay. I have made it this ~~with~~ long without her I can move on from this.

November was a blur. There wasn't one person that sat next to me, but I was doing better. By now I was a full day volunteer in Special Education.
Things started to get better. I really think things only got better because I took a lot of time off.

December came and I had a surgery. There was a lot of gossip about my normal breast-reduction procedure. Sue actually came over once over winter break, but that was the last time; we ever had a normal conversation. Some of the kids were just so illiterate on their gossip.

"She's getting butt implants."

Still ass-less as ever

"Sex reassignment surgery"

Did you even research the recovery

time on that one? *

"Boob Job"

Close! A for effort! F, for thoughtlessness

"Top Surgery"
Half of you don't even know what that is

It was humiliating coming back in January and having everyone staring at me more so than before my breast reduction. I got asked a lot of inappropriate questions by my classmates. This was something I wanted to keep private. If someone asked, I was just going to say that I lost weight. I wasn't ashamed of my surgery, I just felt that it was my right to have a secret. I guess I was wrong. It was so upsetting because in high school things spread like mono so everyone knew, I was treated differently. One of my teachers even made a joke in class about 'top heavy' fractions. My classmates stared at me and gawked. I personally didn't think the joke was very funny. I thought it was offensive, rude and overall very intrusive

In Leadership class, not much changed. I still had no one to sit with. I did presentations in class, but I never had a classmate who wanted to genuinely be my partner. My teacher always had to add me to a group or I worked alone. (Never by choice) It was most definitely not my favorite thing. I just wanted to be included in the conversation. Be liked and accepted by my peers. February was hard for me. I started missing more school and becoming more and more depressed. It was rare to find a day where I wasn't crying in my room alone. I was sad and lonely and there was nothing I could do.

At the end of February, I was working at a table fundraising during lunch with this boy in class and he was just plain mean to me. He called me a 'retard' and that my ideas were dumb. I just didn't get it... He was sarcastic to others, but it seemed like he just really did not like me. I felt so small. I was on social media; the site where you can only use 140 characters and send out blurbs about your day. I thought to myself there must be something going on in his life that made him lash out at me and say those hurtful words. I scrolled through his pictures and right before my very eyes, I saw myself. There was a picture of me taken without my consent. Might I add? It wasn't flattering at all. It was a picture of me standing in front of the classroom by the teacher talking being very expressive with my hand movements. (I like to talk with my hands)

It was captioned verbatim "Shes hella fake" I looked at it again. The picture was taken October 29th I just had never seen it before. I went to my room and cried for the rest of the day and didn't get out of bed during that three day weekend. I showed my mom the picture and she was done. She was sick and tired of me being a moving target in class. We agreed we

were going to show the teacher the picture. I returned to school that Monday. I went straight to the leadership room and said: 'this isn't okay' she agreed and said "I will email the counselor and we can schedule a meeting." We ended up not having a meeting with the counselor. My teacher was called into the principal's office. The principal spoke with my classmate and had the picture removed. No suspension. No consequence.

"He's not the only problem. The entire class is mean to me." I then explained my falling out with Sue. The principal nodded a lot. #JustLikeaBobblehead

"Here's your homework. Write a personal statement with exact dates and we will work something out."

I went home and wrote that personal statement 4 pages non-stop crying and having grammatical errors. I let some of my para-educator friends read it. They were shocked. I brought it down to the principal. I was later interrogated that day. And when I say interrogated. I mean I felt attacked like I was on trial.

"How do you know these people said this about you?"

I was just shocked this was an issue handled so unprofessionally. No empathy in the tones of the voice. A football coach vouched for my classmate's character. That was that. I never heard about that issue again. I never even got an apology from the kid. My step-dad made an appointment to speak with the principal to discuss all of the issues and bullying.

At this point there was an in school separation order placed against Sue and I. We were not to speak to each other. Sue and her mother requested this. It was interesting being that we were in the same leadership class. I guess that's the school system for you.

Please, someone explain how a no-contact order works in a class based on teamwork is supposed to work.

The Original Personal Statement: Below is the statement I wrote back in February. I was distraught when I had to type this! Notice some of the grammatical errors and parts I can't even understand. That my friends is pure rage and sadness,

Because of the constant bullying I received, it has been very hard for me to go to leadership class. I still do every day. I keep things to myself and I do just take the torment because I feel it's easier. I have been harassed and bullied so much that I cannot give you many exact dates. Most of the dates I have taken are from my journals. I apologize in advance that these dates are mostly formatted in the time frames of months. I have put up with a lot of this high school bullying for a very long time but now that I have discovered there is a picture saying that I am "Hella Fake" I decided enough is enough. I can only take so much.

In advanced leadership, I have endured quite a lot of harassment. The kids just don't seem to like me and to think me being genuinely kind is an act. I have been told by several members of the class that I am fake. I have heard countless remarks regarding my sexual orientation, rumors of being very promiscuous when in reality I have never had a boyfriend. To begin with I would just like to clarify I hate confrontation I am definitely a lover and not a fighter. This bullying began in September 2014 right as school began. My previous best friend Sue and I had a falling out. We are no longer friends but for the most part she is cordial towards me. I was really excited for leadership this year. I took it as a sophomore and finally felt accepted and liked, in fact I found my first group of friends in leadership. So being that I had such a wonderful experience last year, I was thrilled to be taking it again Sue and I had a falling out like I mentioned previously. I was well liked the first day of leadership. Afterwards rumors were spread that I was fake and a terrible person by Sue It was even said that I was spreading rumors about her when in reality I am only in two actual classes 3$^{rd.}$ and 4th period. I am here to do my work, and that's it. I don't talk poorly about people because I hate being talked about. This caused the leadership class to turn on me being that she is so well liked and popular. September was also the month when I published my book. Classmates of mine gave me a very tough time about it. There wasn't anyone in my class that supported my books except for Dan and John and of course Betty I was teased for it "Ms. Author" thinks she's better than us, "Madeleine writes a book and now she thinks she's "Hot shit". People seem to think that I have an agenda about everything. I only do things for praise and a response. I wrote my books because I wanted to. No one forced me, I just wanted to do something. I just had an idea nothing more. I don't have an agenda. These students in my class think they know me when in reality they don't give me the time of day.

Around October is when things really started taking a turn for the worst. People would roll their eyes when I would speak. I never had someone sit next to me in class the entire semester I still don't have anyone sitting next to me. It gets quite lonely. It honestly hurt my feelings. I have pitched ideas and they were denied the second I would raise my hand. I consider myself a very strong person, I know what kind of person I am and don't usually let things bother me. However this daily torment finally got to me. I dropped the class for about a week in October, but because of how much leadership impacted me I decided to stay. I thought things would change but unfortunately they only got worse. This is when rumors were spread about my sexual orientation. Sue and I were beginning to talk again at the time. But that reunion was cut short because two girls Margo and Tina started giving her a tough time about being civil towards me "Oh your girlfriend is looking for you".. Because of that rumor a lot of the girls don't like being around me because they think I am some sort of predator. This eventually caused us to quit working on repairing our friendship. Which is unfortunate because she meant a lot to me. Because of the bad vibes Sue and I shared this a reason of why I think the class does not like me. Betty had Sue and I down during 6th period on October 22nd to hash out our differences after I opened up to her saying that I wanted things to get better and the reason I left was because of the poor treatment I was receiving. She immediately apologized and asked me what I wanted her to do. I told her that I didn't know so she decided that things don't get better unless we talk about it. Around October is when Adam really started to be degrading and rude to me. I would hear him whisper rumors about me To K. I never really listened in on what they were saying because frankly I could care less. I was honestly in so much pain from the decay of my friendship with Sue. I was physically really sick for a while from it. I couldn't bear to listen to the rumors or gossip even if I wanted to. I think I would have broken down

November, things really started to blow over. I mean there weren't many rumors about me but the kids still couldn't stand the sight of me. I continued to be nice to everyone because that is just how I was brought up. Even some of the kids who I thought were leadership kids who were very kind to me in the beginning turned on me Hannah and Jessica no longer received acknowledgement from either girls and you could tell it pained them to talk to me. Alicia even spread a rumor that Betty didn't want me to be at an event

December I had a breast reduction, I need to point out the only person I confided that in was Sue back over the summer. I wanted to keep it pretty private. Being that she was my best friend I couldn't tell her. There were rumors spread that I was using my excess breast tissue for butt implants. I know these rumors had to start in Leadership. As I stated previously I confided in Sue back over the summer when I had my consultation. I cannot pin that on her per say because personally I don't want to believe that I was betrayed when I told someone something that private. When I returned to school everyone found out. I didn't care because to be quite honest I was the happiest I had ever been in a long time. My breasts identified me throughout freshman, sophomore and a

Portion of junior year. I was known as Madeleine with the big boobs I cannot name everyone who said something because a lot of the rude remarks were just jabs at me and mostly I put up with several gawks, and stares at my chest which unfortunately I am very used to. People would ask if it was true or why I did it. At this point I did not care. I would respond with a "yes" and when the students would ask why I had the procedure done all I would say was that "My surgeon wouldn't have done it if it weren't medically necessary." That response was the way to usual keep people quiet. I have to commend Dan for actually being very kind about my surgery and being so genuinely interested and concerned about my health. Being that I am a running start student, I have a lot of spare time on my hands so I try to be involved and help out in Leadership as much as I can. Ask anyone who likes me I am always the first to volunteer for a project, or raise my hand. I volunteered to help Sue, *Tom*, and *Morgan* with The winter assembly. I wanted to make sure they were aware that if they needed anything to let me know because I worked on it last year. K responded with "I don't want your help, and we don't need your help" to paraphrase for lack of a kinder word she told me to buzz off.

January was quite a blur. I just remember rumors coming back about my sexual identity about how that I was born a man something along the lines of that. Quite shockingly that isn't the first time I heard that. But other than rumors about me being promiscuous I was told by a number of people how cheap I looked because I enjoy getting my nails done and enjoying a spray tan every once in a while. This is where people began once again to tell me how fake I was.

On Friday January 30th that is when I found the picture. Ada*m* was not very kind to me while tabling for the Adam Building Wells Music booth at lunch. I scrolled through his twitter to see if there was a reason why he was being so terrible towards me. It was just a lot of eye rolls when I'd associate with the SLC kids as well as their para educators. Whom of which the majority of the kids in leadership would not associate with. They tell me how 'retarded' I am. Personally I just think that is hate speech. Anyway, I was truly hurt by the picture because I think that is new level of bullying. It's one thing to tweet anonymously about an annoying girl who's fake in leadership but the fact of the matter is I was identified. I know the photo was from October and that is long gone. I think of it in the perspective of other students. Not everyone would handle it in the way I did handle it. The outcome could have been extremely different and lucky for I know who I am, because if I posted something like that and the outcome was fatal I don't think I would be able to go on. I couldn't fathom hurting someone that bad. Joke or not whatever his intentions were the bottom line is I was hurt. In a sense I feel violated. I know it's a picture of my back, and no one liked the picture. I have nothing against Adam I am just really hurt by what went down. When I saw that picture I cried. I felt really low and disgusting. At first I did think that maybe it was me. I was at fault and I thought of all the ways that I could change to be less fake but I realized I wasn't the problem. That following Monday I was just very upset I wasn't myself. I just didn't understand why Adam would do something like that. I just worry not only for myself, but for him. If he continues this the odds aren't going to end up on his paper. I feel this age we are vulnerable enough as is and cyberbullying does a lot of damage to self-esteem. I just really want him to be aware of the damage he caused. I would rather him learn about the dangers of bullying rather than giving him a suspension or any other consequence. I know my bullying situation isn't as bad as others but if he were to walk a day in my shoes and not be treated kindly by the leadership kids, or have a place to sit at lunch I think his outlook would change tremendously. Knowledge is powerful and I truly do feel that no matter what his intentions were he needs to be aware. I have nothing against Adam personally. He just made a dumb choice. We all have. In fact I have heard such wonderful things about him, I hope he can learn from this and not hurt anyone else. I am not asking for a friendship I am just asking for the respect that I give to him to be returned to me.

I spend a lot my time with the SLC kids I volunteer in the classroom for a good couple of hours a daily. I do enjoy my time with these kids they are the highlight of my day! They benefit me more so than I am told that I benefit them. One of the main reasons I do work in the classroom is because my mom, is a para educator in Ms. Blanks's class. Another reason I spend a majority of my time in there is because I do enjoy the kids. They make me really happy! Finally I just know that I am not going to be judged or treated in a hostile manner around the kids because I know the paras and Ms. Blank enjoy having me there. The students enjoy having me in class too. The opinions of my leadership classmates are less than favorable in regards to my reasoning for spending time with the kids. I have been told by a number of people that "no one really likes the kids and you have other reasons to be in the classroom." I started having lunch with Emily. She is a junior in Ms. Blank's room we have lunch together every Friday as of now. I have overheard that I am only having lunch with her for 'attention'. I don't want attention I actually hate attention put on me. I don't understand why everyone would think I have ulterior motives and I find it quite sad that every time I do something nice there has to be that I have some sort of agenda for doing so. I don't want praise, or attention. I just want to be the best person I can be. I just feel like I am treated in a manner where I am talked down to. The kids are very condescending towards me in leadership. They seem to think I don't know anything.

I just feel bad everything has come down to me having to write a personal statement about my experience. My classmates don't give a chance to let me share something. I am honestly shamed if I talk about anything that excites me or that I am interested in. I am just hurt. I believe that we don't care unless we are aware, and if the leadership students did know that there are consequences for the actions I think things would be better. I don't know why of all the classes, leadership class is the one that turned on me and made me feel unsafe. I would like these students to be held accountable for the sadness and frustration I was put through. Nobody wants to feel unsafe and uncomfortable in school yet I did. That being said I do need to point out that there are a few kids who genuinely have their heart in the right place Dan, who always makes a point to say hello to me, as well as John who is soft spoken, but is so kind.

Last semester, Ryan was amazing towards me and just added comfort into such a hostile environment. Is Betty also incredible, she is good about checking in to see whether or not I am ok. It's just so sad that

All in all, these little things add up. I have experienced name calling, cattiness from the girls, as well as the boys too. Ultimately I think this rooted from a sour ending to a friendship. Leadership is way different than what is was last year. I like everyone else just want to feel liked. I may carry myself differently and maybe I do come across fake. But the fact of the matter is I just want to be accepted and treated with kindness, respect, and dignity. I can handle name calling, people questioning my sexual orientation, and general rudeness. I shouldn't have to handle it or face it but I do. I do every day with a smile on my face. I try my best to kill people with kindness. I still stay hello and I am cordial and decent to every student in that class even the ones who do not particularly care for me. I realize that not everyone is going to like me but I do believe like everyone else, I do deserve to feel safe in a classroom which is supposed to have an agenda of inclusion and kindness.

Personally, I thought that personal statement included enough information. To the principals it didn't.

I returned with an issue in March. I reached out to one classmate for the sake of privacy, we'll call him John. I listed John in the personal statement, as someone who could be a confidant. I also listed another boy Dan down as a witness I had asked Dan if he would be willing and comfortable to talk to the principal for me. He agreed. I emailed that principal asking to have a meeting.

during 5th period. That way, no one would know. I also requested for another principal who knew me better to be present as well. She replied and said that 4th period works for her. I agreed with hesitation, but I thought everything would be okay since I asked for discretion.

No discretion was used that day. Let's just say that principal ignored that request pulling the both of us out of class personally. Then continuing to have me sit on a bench in front of the office. Where they continued to pull out student after student from my class.

"Did you call Madeleine a bitch?"

"No, I like Madeleine."
"Ok, go back to class."

"This raises a major red flag in your direction Madeleine. Makes me think you aren't telling the truth."

This continued about 10-15 more times. I am

not going to get too deep into this meeting. It hurts way too much! After one straight hour of being berated and torn down as well as saying I made it up. I returned to my class. My eyes were bloodshot and my mascara was all over my face. I grabbed my purse and left for the day. I walked... or should I say ran home in hysterics and had my mom pick me up on the street corner. This day could easily go down as the day I hit rock bottom. I was so hurt and sick. I began gaining weight like nobody's business being the heaviest I have ever been. I also went from an A in my Algebra 2 class to an F all in the matter of weeks. My attendance was spottier than ever. I just didn't care. I just wanted to stay in bed all day. I faked being happy for a very long time. I got really good at it. Looking at me, you wouldn't be able to tell I was dying inside. I always looked put together right down to a few stray eyebrow hairs. I was always smiling and laughing. Only those who were close to me knew how difficult everything was for me.

April and May are sort of a blur to me except for one thing. After losing clumps of my hair and crying every day and feeling so alone. I withdrew from the class. I decided I was done. I hated it so much. I hated leadership class! A class based on inclusion, acceptance, and strong character. These were an elite group of kids who were compassionate and set apart from the rest. These were the example students. And the kind kids bullied me. The kids who promote anti-bullying. Oh the irony! Bullied by the nice kids. I was broken. I never thought I would get better or feel better. I was sick. Physically, emotionally, and mentally. I let one class have so much power over me. However, despite the negativity in my life I made a conscious choice to be happy. I had all the power in the world to get out of my funk. So I did. Leaving that class was the best choice for me. I stuck it out way longer than I should have.

Even though, I withdrew from the class that caused so much distress, I still wasn't happy. Like every high school student, I just wanted to fit in. So I did the thing that any other incoming senior in school would do... I applied for the leadership program again. Leadership was such a large part of my identity, I felt empty without it. I felt lost without the team building exercises and poster making. It sounds so stupid, but I joined because I felt as everything was taken away from me. I just wanted some control!

In June, I put up a fight to be included in yearbook signings and saying goodbye to my friends in Special Education where I spent most of my year!

I thought it was all over for me. My record was blemished. I was sad and lonely. This was quite possibly the year from hell. I lost my best friend. I lost my safe space.

I lost it all. I would never wish what happened to me on anyone... Not even Sue. This was such a dark and miserable time. As I, sit here wiping my tears. I can only smile. I finished my junior year. I ended my year with a completely new group of people. I learned so much about myself this year. I did it... I survived. ♥

Dear Diary,

I'm free! School's out for summer and I couldn't feel any better about it! I have realized how extremely lucky I am. I have so many amazing people in my life. Reflecting on this year really makes me realize that everything in my life happens for a reason! I am overwhelmed with all of the good people who have come into my life recently. Without all of this ▓▓▓▓▓ drama, I don't think I would be the person I am today. I am 100% fully myself. No regrets or doubts. I couldn't be happier with the outcome of this year.

58

I have
never felt so
speciall or loved
in 2015 school year
end fantastically
I am Free!

I wrote that diary entry on the last day of school. I am so happy to be able to say all of the things I did. I have realized that I do not need negativity in my life. I wish I realized it much sooner… but I guess better late than never. I am now in an environment where things can only get better.

High school is a scary time. I know how hard we all want to be accepted and liked. It would be easier to follow the cookie cutter mold that is expected. Let me tell you a secret, fitting into the mold isn't always the best option. *GASP* I know bear with me, break down the barriers and be authentic. The mold isn't always valuable. Why do you think famous paintings are so expensive, and custom made shoes cost the most? It's because they are one of a kind!

Chapter 4: The Five Stages of Bullying

Like anything in life there is going to be steps and pieces. These stages are the natural way you react and feel when going through something major. Just like puberty, bullying is major! When my classmates bullied me, I went through many stages of how I felt. These five were the most prominent. We are going to take a ride on the wild side and visit my not so sweet emotions. My diary entries really show my emotions better than any chart. Damn, this is literally an open book.

Diary Entries

I handle my emotions best through writing. My diary blurbs give a clear idea of how I was feeling each and every day in school.

Diary Entry 3: 1/29/15 — Late Night Thoughts

> 1/29/15
> Dear Diary,
> Lately I have been asking myself
> will I ever find happiness? Right now
> I don't know what's going on with
> I am miserable. I hate getting up
> the morning, I can't sleep, I can't
> in eat. I don't feel good about
> elf. I feel fat and ugly.
> feel stupid and worthless. I am just
> myself. I just want to sleep, I don't
> to go to school or anything
> wrong with me? Why don't I have
> e friend? I am so nice. Why does
> ne hate me? Why am I not
> like the other girls? Why don't I
> myself anymore? Will I be able
> again I have all of these questions,
> but yet I have zero answers
> know anymore
>   - Madeleine

Diary Entry 4: 1/30/15 – "Need a Friend"

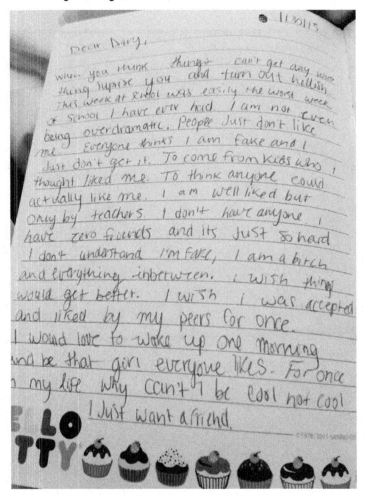

1/30/15

Dear Diary,

When you think things can't get any worse thing suprise you and turn out hellish. This week at school was easily the worst week of school I have ever had I am not even being overdramatic. People just don't like me everyone thinks I am fake and I just don't get it. To come from kids who I thought liked me. To think anyone could actually like me. I am well liked but only by teachers. I don't have anyone I have zero friends and its just so hard I don't understand I'm fake, I am a bitch and everything inbetween. I wish things would get better. I wish I was accepted and liked by my peers for once. I would love to wake up one morning and be that girl everyone likes. For once in my life why can't I be cool not cool I just want a friend.

I can whole heartedly say "I give up". I am done with everything. I am mentally, and emotionally sick. This is my cry for help. This is my shot to get better.

Madeleine's Happiness

It all goes down hill. I am done.

Madeleine

Diary Entry 6: 2/15/15 — "I can't"

I don't know what to do with myself. I don't feel good anymore. I can barely keep food down, I don't feel I pretty, or smart I have beaten down to a point where I just feel empty.

I just want to go to school and go home. Hell I don't even want to go to school anymore But I have to keep going.

I have to stay strong But its so hard to be positive when I don't matter and I am worthless to someone else. If people knew how I felt, they'd be shocked or would they. When in reality the only people who care about me is my family. My mom can tell when I am sad but no one else maybe that's a good thing.

Diary Entry 7: 5/20/15 — "The Night"

5/20

Dear Diary,
When something good happens things will always go back to being miserable and sad. Tonight is the night. I have a messy room and swollen, red puffy eyes.
I am going to be extremely blunt. I am depressed. I need help but I cannot fathom the idea of asking for it. I think it's finally setting in. I feel guilty after every breath I take and word I say because there are people who would be better and happier.
I am sad beyond belief. I think of all the people who don't like me and realize is their even a point anymore? Is there a reason to fight with myself day in an day out? NO.. so why do I ev bother at all. I feel I have no purpose and I have lost what makes me well me. I can't live like this anymore. How do I know next year will be any better?

1. "Why Me?"

I did not understand why something this bad happen to me. What did I do to deserve this horrible treatment? This is where the pity party and the confusion begins.

2. "Is it me?"

I thought it was me. There had to be a reason why nobody liked me. Was it the way I spoke? Did I come across rude? Was it my body, or my hair? Did it have to do with how much I cared?

3. "I hate myself!"

It had to be me. If nobody else likes me, I can't like myself. I don't deserve friends.

I don't deserve happiness because I am worthless. They are right about me.

4. "It's not my fault"

I am not worthless. I know that I am special and kind. I am beautiful inside and out. They don't like me. That is their problem, not mine. The only thing I can do is be kind to myself. Move on with your life these people are holding you back.

5. "I am going to be okay."

I built up all of this negative energy. Now here I am getting my mojo back, and feeling good about myself. I am on cloud nine and now it's my time to thrive! This is also known as recovery and it will take some time.

These emotions running through your body are all normal. I spent a long time struggling with being bullied. The school year ended and I am still recovering. I have a long road ahead of me to get back to the place where I am fully myself again. But I have to make it clear; you have to choose happiness. It's not something that comes to you. You have to fight for it and create it yourself. I am creating my happy.

You have options on how you handle these emotions. You can let them take over your life and make you miserable like I did, or you can fight back and allow yourself to be happy.

It's absolutely natural for you to feel sad. It's even healthy to feel bad you're human. But what isn't healthy is for you to feel hopeless and helpless. I am not a doctor, but these feelings you are experiencing can be depression or lead to depression. I didn't seek help. I was embarrassed. I didn't put my feelings first. I eventually overcame these feelings, but I didn't take care of myself. As I mentioned before I gained weight, and I even lost clumps of hair from all of the stress and daily torture I put myself through day in and day out.

There is help for those who are experiencing extremely high doses of sadness. I advise anyone feeling this way to see a doctor. This could be the difference of seven sad days down to four.

I am in recovery. I still do have bad days. But they are necessary and healthy bad days. I am happier than I was 6 months ago. I am happier than I was 4 weeks ago. I am getting better. I know you will get better too ♥

Back in chapter 3, I discussed my story and how I tried to get help from others. It didn't work in my favor, but that doesn't mean it has to work out that way for you. You have established you're being bullied. So who do you turn to? Who is going to be your best asset? Who is going to have your back? It has been stated in a lot of bullying material and curriculums that you need to tell an adult. Pretty vague if you ask me. You need to have some criteria for who you are going to open up to. Opening up puts you in a very exposed position. Butt-Naked exposure. You're practically a centerfold. So what criteria should you base it on?

Chapter 5: What do I do?

When you are a teenager, everything can feel like the end of the world. So we have clearly come to the realization you are being bullied. So now what, do you just live with it? Not at all. Here is how to handle it.

Back in chapter 3, I discussed my story and how I tried to get help from others. It didn't work in my favor, but that doesn't mean it has to work out that way for you. You have established you're being bullied. So who do you turn to now? Who is going to be your best bet? Who is going to have your back and be your buddy?

Who Do I Tell?

1. The teacher who runs the class where you are being bullied.

   A teacher's job not only is to educate, but to protect. It is their job to make sure people are treating each other respectfully. They want you to feel comfortable.

2. A trusted adult.

This can be a parent, or relative. A teacher even a counselor. Your coach, whoever makes you happy.

3. The principal

It is their school. They have a handbook full of rules about bullying. They get paid to do more than monitor the lunch rooms and spin in their swivel chairs.

4. A friend

Choose wisely on this one. Friends are tricky. News travels fast.

When picking someone to confide in. Go through an application process. Really narrow it down to the best possible person. I mean you don't get hired at a job for having a pretty face... You have to possess skills!

1. Look for a teacher who has empathy. Does their classroom syllabus from the beginning of the year have specific rules about bullying, certain words. (R-word, N-word, etc.) Practicing decency to all? How about respecting others, regardless of sexual orientation, religion, beliefs, gender identity, etc. Does this teacher fight the good fight? Are you comfortable in the classroom?

2. Is the adult willing to listen?

3. Do you trust this person?

4. Is this friend close with your bully?

5. Does your principal treat everyone equally?

If you have the luxury of having a teacher to confide in, do. They can keep an eye on the class. They see you every day and can see how you are feeling. I was very lucky to have a teacher looking out for me.

If you can tell someone at home, do. It's great to get a few people together who can vouch for your mental health status. Who better to help with that than someone who lives with you?

HINT: When finding someone at school, look for a GSA (Gay-Straight-Alliance) or anti-bullying club adviser. They deal with these issues often and will be great advocates for you. These are the people who are fighting the good fight. They will help you. Their goals are to make everyone feel comfortable.

That is a mouthful of information let's break it down into a simpler format

1. Empathy
2. Listen
3. Trust
4. Friends
5. Equally

There are people who want to help you. However, you have to be careful on who you choose to help you. In my situation. I didn't narrow it down. I chose obvious choices like the teacher, the principal, and classmates. I was not shown any empathy. I was not listened to. I did not trust, and I was not treated equally.

Lucky for me, I didn't tell any friends,

You should be able to turn to your principals and teachers for help. It shouldn't have to be this big ordeal to get help but sometimes it is. I am not saying don't tell your principal or teacher. Just please find someone you know who is going to do right by you. Be cautious this is a very big deal. Take the time and really delve down.

When going through my own process of sharing my story; there were many people who had sympathetic ears, but there were other people who just wanted to listen. What I mean by that is there were people who truly cared, but there was also many people who just wanted to hear, what was coming out of my mouth.

Are you confident, in your confidant?

Take the quiz below. To find out if your confidant is a good match. Answer truthfully and check the box that most relates to your confidant.

1. Do you know this person well? (Friend, teacher you know, etc.)

 Yes or No

2. Does this person have integrity?

(Will they do the right thing?)

 Yes or No

3. Are you comfortable talking to this person? (Will you feel right telling this person your situation?)

 Yes or No

4. Are you confident in their competence? (Answer yes if you answered yes to all of the above?)

 Yes or No

If you answered mostly yes: This is most-likely someone good to confide in.

If you answered mostly no: This is probably not your best choice. Try to find someone else
If your answers are somewhere in between: Think long and hard about who you confide in. Rethink your choice.

How Do I Tell?

I am so happy you were able to find the right person to open up to. Now it's time to have the conversation. Let me be one of the first people to tell you how proud I am. Opening up is brave. You are courageous!

1. "I have something really important to talk to you about. Could we talk sometime soon?"

You are being direct and showing the person you have something to say.

2. "I have been bullied for a
   while now. I just don't know
   what to do."

You are being blunt. Be honest, that is the

only way this person is going to be able to help

you. Give them names and tell them exactly

what's going on. How you are feeling. If you

think you are depressed or sad. Anything and

everything you say will help them help you.

3. "Can you help me?"

You've put it out there. You have opened up and said that you need help. Listen to them take every idea into mind.

Ok, I made it seem much simpler on the pages. It's hard to open up and be defenseless. But you know what's even harder? Being bullied.

Bite the bullet and open up. If you have to write down notes. Do it. Do what works for you. Whatever you think will make you feel more prepared, then do it. Just know by telling your story you are helping others. Telling someone is going to help make it better.

Keep an open conversation. Communicate your feelings. All that truly matters is that you say what's on your mind. You are not weak for showing emotion. Trust me, it's a tough conversation to have. You are putting down the barrier and being open. Just think of it this way.

You are **one step closer to solving your problem.**

I am so proud of you

Handling things

yourself

So you have asked for help? That's amazing! But how do you handle things on your own? How do you stand up for yourself? There are so many ways that you can diffuse a situation.

For me, I liked to use humor. Being that I am an active ally of the LGBT+ community. I get lots of rude and invasive questions asked on my social media pages. One night in particular, I just got really fed up being asked about my sexuality, that I got sassy.

Are you gay? I read your books and I am just curious because you talk a lot about equality and tolerance, but especially for gay people. Don't you feel it is your duty to be out to help some of the readers that you relate to?

Madeleine Gasperi Hi,
I understand your curiosity in regards to my sexual orientation. I must be really interesting! To answer your question I am straight, I like men... maybe a bit too much I should probably see a doctor about it :). That doesn't mean I can't appreciate a beautiful woman though. It's not being gay or bi or anything it's being kind. I do tell girls that they are gorgeous because they are, not because I have a burning passion to take one home with me. Secondly, I talk about equality and tolerance because it is now 2015 and there is still people using the word 'gay' to mean stupid and people with special needs are still called the R-word and that is not ok! I do relate to my readers, but not in that sense. Closet is really an umbrella term don't you think? I mean maybe I'm closeted in the sense that I have a huge crush on John Stamos... That's not a secret. Thank you for question I hope that cleared things up for you.
Warm Regards,
Madeleine Gasperi

I was honest, upfront, and I used humor.

It's like a secret weapon. No one ever

expects someone who was put down to be

silly about it. It's the element of surprise.

Like raisins in a carrot cake... That's not as fun of a surprise. You can be sarcastic and witty to a bully.

Bullies don't think that far in advance for a humorous come back. They think that you aren't going to fight back

Maybe humor isn't your forte. The possibilities are endless. You can be the bigger person and ignore it. Or maybe you want to be forward and tell the bully to "Knock it off!" You can walk away. That's not cowardly, it's grown up and mature.

How you choose to handle a bully is all up to you. The main objective is that said bully leaves you alone.

So bust out your joke books or your prep books to <u>outsmart</u>. Do what you feel is right. As long as it is not reckless violence. I do not condone that. The only reason violence should be an option is for self-defense.

Never be mean either. There is a big difference between sarcasm, humor, wit, and being mean. Humor is smart, being mean is hurtful.

You don't want to become a bully yourself. You are just making the cycle spread more like a bad case of mono and we don't want that!

Chapter 6: Confidence

Confidence is easy to lose and hard to gain.

A teacher of mine in the tenth grade used to give us a pep talk before we would take tests in class. "I am good enough. I am smart enough, and gosh darn it people like me!" He knew that instilling confidence in his class would help us do better and feel better on test days. It's true, our success has a lot to do with how we feel.

When being bullied I know it can feel like all the color and everything good has been sucked out of the world; but let me tell you confidence is key. Finding your voice can get you out of dark times.

Bullies look for people with low self-esteem because they are easier to put down. It's a fact.

Confidence has to do with many aspects including how we treat ourselves, how we speak about ourselves; how we let others treat us. It's just a circle of self-worth.

Do You Have The Confidence Key?

Do you have the keys to be confident or do you think poorly of yourself? Take the quiz below with honest answers to get an understanding on whether or not youkan unlock the door to happiness.

1. Do you pick apart your flaws?
   YES/NO/SOMETIMES

2. Do you talk poorly aboutyourself?
   YES/NO/SOMETIMES

3. Are you proud of yourself?
    YES/NO/SOMETIMES

4. Do you feel less than your peers?
   YES/NO/SOMETIMES

If you picked yes and sometimes answers, we have some work to do. You are a beautiful person. You have every right to confidence. You can do it. You will be more confident.

Confidence is tricky. I will be the first
to admit it, I hate talking about myself.
It makes me uncomfortable. I will feel
bad for eating a candy bar or a bag of
chips. I will get discouraged when I
don't look good in a top or get a bad
grade. I will write diary entries on how
I wish I were prettier, or smarter.
Confidence is a journey. It derives from
acceptance.

Accept that there are going to be days
where you don't want to look in the
mirror and accept that are going to be
days where you know you look good.
It's all about finding that balance.

Accept that there are going to be people
who don't like you. (Still working on that
one)

Accept that in order to live a full life you
have to accept yourself. It is your job to
be yourself. Find the strength to love
yourself all of you. Rock what you've got

You are born with certain attributes whether they are physical, emotional or romantic. You can't change your skin color, or ethnicity. You have no control over whom you fall in love with or who you want to be. You can't change what makes you unique! The more you draw attention to the things you aren't accepting, the more people will notice and use them against you.

A: Appreciate what you are

C: Care about yourself

C: Create a kind environment

E: Explore what you love

P: Practice self-love
T: Take time for yourself
A: Allow yourself to feel good
N: Notice what you are good at
C: Change how you feel about yourself.
E: Engage in positivity

Confidence is a powerful thing. It can make others leave you alone. When people see that you are content with yourself, they are less likely to bother you. It is important to be confident and to always put your best foot forward.

Be content with the content

Confidence isn't loving every part of yourself. Confidence is accepting your insecurities and being proud of who you are. There are days when I feel less than my best. Sometimes you just have to enhance what you are feeling with a positive attitude.

Faking it so you can make It

Walk like you own the place, Smile like you are on the red carpet. Stand up as straight as a board. Confidence is all about how you carry yourself. If you believe that you are confident, eventually you will be confident. Others will think you are confident and proud of yourself too.

Look Good. Feel Good. Do Good.

I have learned one of the best ways to get out of a funk is to put on my favorite outfit, do my hair and makeup. I always fix up on test days because I feel good so I do well. Put time into yourself. You deserve those 10 extra minutes to put a little pride in your stride.

Wash away Your insecurities

I always feel my best after a shower. I feel rejuvenated. I truly get a clean slate and a recharge.

Soak your muscles in hot water and reflect. I along with many others think best in the shower. Also, you really get to take a long private look at yourself. It's probably one, the only times you really get to see yourself. Find what you like, and see what you do not like. You are allowed no to like something about yourself, and if you're not happy you have the right to change it.

Exercise Positivity

Going on a nice run and blasting my music just gets my mood set. I feel accomplished, empowered, and proud that I did something good for my health. Running is great for your body as well as your mind. I don't know what it is (not a doctor yet), but I just feel really good after a run. I just feel on top of the world and in control.

Swimming is also a great stress reliever. It works almost all of your muscles. Maybe you are a sports person, (I don't do balls) It doesn't matter what you do because the point is to be active!

Nothing fixes your mood better than a good old fashioned pep talk

Sometimes all it takes to get out of a funk and get through the day is a few positive words. One thing that helped me get through many hard days was writing. I would write letters to myself and say anything and everything I could in my power to build myself back up after being torn down.

On the next few pages, I would like you to write your very own pep talk, as I have done for myself on the next page. And whenever you are feeling down on yourself, come back and look at it. It's a pick me up that may work for you. Give it a shot!

Writing Your Pep Talk

When writing a pep talk or a positive note, here are a few do's and Don'ts

Do: Speak highly of yourself.

Don't: Compare yourself to others.

Do: Write down how you feel.

Don't: Put blame on anyone.

Do: Write solutions that will make you happier.

Don't: Dwell. You have a chance in the letter to clarify that things aren't going your way, but don't make the whole letter about that. Dwelling ruins every shot at you becoming well.

Do: Make a plan on what you're going to do.

Don't: Be afraid to get emotional.

Dear 2015 Madeleine,

This letter is for when you feel like quitting or you're not good enough. You need to know how incredible you are. I know how hard it is for you Right now. Your Junior year could easily be compared to Middle School. It's Okay that you don't fit in. You are way more mature and I know how hard it is. You feel alone so so alone. You are not alone Madeleine there are so many people who care and love you. You Just haven't found them yet. You Struggle and have a lot of battles within yourself let things go because even though it may seem like its the end of the world in the moment it won't be as big of a deal in a few weeks. When things get tough ask for help. Take a few days off of School and recover. You're smart and it won't hurt you.

My Pep Talk Pick Me Up

When you find your inner confidence, you tend to learn a lot about yourself. You find your strength. When you finally embrace all that you are, that is when you are living to your fullest potential.

In this world, we put so many people on pedestals and dream of looking like and having what they have, but the truth is...We need to love ourselves as we are! In this next activity, I am putting your confidence to the test.

It's time to get uncomfortable and start loving yourself from the inside out.

It's time to exercise... Don't worry, I won't make you run... It's time to work out your mind

Recite these to yourself, when you are feeling down on yourself. Remember how great you are!

DISCLAIMER I am not a poet and I know these are cheesy! But you know what they say about cheese and confidence. "It's Gouda to believe in yourself!"

Mirror, Mirror On the Wall

I am a strong and confident person. I am beautiful inside and out.

My favorite thing about myself is

_____(Physical). I am

great at_____ (talent).

I am_____

(adjective). I may not like everything about myself every day. I may not be great at everything. That is not what defines me. But that is what makes me, me and sets me apart from the rest making me my very best!

I Am

There is so much more to me than who I appear to be. I am proud of the person I am. I love myself. I am great. I am special. I am unique. I am_____(name)

Chapter 7: Blossom, Succeed and Thrive.

Congratulations! You have found your voice. You found the confidence to leave a negative situation. <u>It can only get better from here!</u> This is the time to be your best self.

After coming out of such a negative situation mine; being bullied, I knew I never wanted anyone to go through what I did. I knew I wanted to give a voice to the voiceless. That is why I am sitting here typing up my story, just so I can help you. In order to make the best out of something negative, you must find your passion. Something you love to do. A passion is something you genuinely care about. Find your hobbies. Find what makes you happy, to wake up and begin your day. For me, writing is a hobby I turned into a passion. I knew that I was destined to be a writer... but not just a writer, an advocate, and an ally. This is me making my mark on the world. Maybe for you, your hobby is baking. Bake a cake of positivity. CHEESY, I KNOW. But seriously find how baking will put the icing on the cake for someone else. Maybe you can bake for fundraisers; you can volunteer to bake for the homeless. If sports are your thing, find out how you can volunteer to teach sports to people with disabilities. Convince others not to throw in the towel! If you like art, find how you can get involved with outreach programs who use art as a creative outlet to help those who are struggling.

Thriving is all about finding something you like to do and making a positive impact on others. It won't be easel, but it will be worth it. Paint your blank canvas with a dream, or a vision something you aspire to be. *NO MORE PUNS MADELEINE* It only takes one person to make a difference. Why not you?

Finding your passions can be difficult. At the time of the bullying I was going through, I spent a lot of time volunteering with the special education students. I only started to have a place to eat my lunch and a place to feel safe. I ended up making some of the best friends and I genuinely care about every single one of the kids I bonded with. I would take each one of them home with me if I could! I love them so much! ♥ They benefited me so much more than I thought they would.

I realized I truly do enjoy working with kids. Not only was I able to eat my lunch in a safe place, I was able to open my eyes and learn about having empathy and more compassion. I was lucky enough to be friends with these kids. I helped a girl learn to write her name and memorize her phone number. That's not even the best part. I was able to overcome my dark time and help someone else at the same time. It's killing two birds with one stone.

And if you don't know what you like to do; try new things!

I urge you to find your passion. Let yourself blossom into the person you are meant to become. Let go of the negativity and thrive. I did it and it was the best decision I made. I am an author at 17; I made a new group of friends. I am making the change by doing what I love!

Find your passion. Find your cause build your empire and your dreams!

Goal Setting

If you are anything like me, you let bullies run your life. I was stuck in a rut where I did not do anything for myself. I accomplished things during this time. I published a couple of books, but I didn't have any goals or ambition. I was so tired that I was on autopilot. I went to class every day and I did well. I just did not put in any extra work. Goal setting it seems pretty self-explanatory, but we are going to do it right. I want you to achieve all you can.

Setting a Goal

1. Identify the goal

   *what do you want to achieve

2. Who is the goal for?

   *If the goal isn't specifically to make you happy. Repeat step one

3. When do you want to achieve this goal?

   *Make sure the time frame is doable.

4. Celebrate

*No matter how small, every single accomplishment is worth celebrating!

Your goals can be anything you want. It can be school related, health related, work related, friend related. Whatever it may be. Set goals. It is important to keep occupied during something as depressing as bullying. Keep occupied, but also alert.

You have to stay motivated.

Chapter 8: Moving on

This was by far my favorite part of my experience, but it was also the hardest of them all; moving on. It's time to let go of all of the negativity in your life.

For me that meant resigning from a program that I knew was doing nothing for me.

Accepting that I wasn't going to be friends with the person that I thought was my best friend. It was hard. Moving on is life changing. You feel a sense of relief. You just weeded all of the drama out of your life. You don't care what others have to say about you.

I felt so strong and liberated. It was the biggest weight lifted off of my shoulders! I was finally free! Free to be happy.

To make something positive out of all of the hardship. I finished that school year with a brand new group of people. I wasn't close to anyone I began my year with. It feels so good not to have someone holding you back. I began living. Back a few months ago, I was merely just existing. I was not happy, I was not healthy. I was hurting and broken. But look at me today. I am writing this to show you it does indeed get better. Slowly but surely all things work out in the end.

The steps I took to be a happy person was first and foremost, leaving the group and exploring myself as an individual. It's frightening. It really is but if there are people who make you feel bad about yourself, or are intentionally hurting you... Get rid of them. Even if that person is your BFF. NEWSFLASH: best friends aren't supposed to treat each other like crap.

They are supposed to be the people who build you up and make you feel good. If they aren't doing that, find new friends. I thought the friendship was going to last forever. Two years with someone feels like forever. Things change, people grow apart and you realize your worth. You understand that you NEED to surround yourself with good, uplifting, and positive people.

Losing that friendship was very hard on me. This was the girl I considered my person. I had other friends, but she was special. We spent a lot of time together. Every weekend was an adventure. She was who I shared my secrets with. Who I had sleepovers with every weekend. Moving on and finding new friends is hard, but it is so worth it. I kept this person around a lot longer than I should have, kind of like an old pilled sweater. It's comfortable, but even though I outgrew it, I still had some desire keep it around.

Sure, I could have used my sweater shaver, but it had holes beyond belief and stains that no amount of bleach or stain remover could get out. It was just more work for me, than it was fashionable or even cute for that matter. #SweatersAreJustLikeFriends

In order to find new friends, you have to put yourself out there in order to let go and make new friends. It's scary, I know. It's terrifying to start over. But we all have to start somewhere. Join clubs, sports, find people with similar interests. It will be a lot easier to move on.

Anyone who brings you down and makes you feel less than is toxic get rid of them before you are brainwashed and think this is okay.

I DON'T CARE WHO IT IS. IT IS NEVER OKAY FOR SOMEONE TO HURT YOU PHYSICALLY, OR EMOTIONALLY. CUT THE CORD NOW!!

Do I have a Toxic Friend?

Is your friend dragging you down? Take the quiz to see if your friend is the best choice to keep around.

1. Are you often the butt of your friends' jokes?

   YES/NO/SOMETIMES

2. Do you ever find yourself crying over something he/she said?
   YES/NO/SOMETIMES

3. Do you dread seeing him/her?

   YES/NO/SOMETIMES

4. Are you more upset than you are happy while they're around?

YES/NO/SOMETIMES

5. Do you worry more about what they think than what you think?

YES/NO/SOMETIMES

6. Do they only talk to you when it is convenient for them?

YES/NO/SOMETIMES

7. Do they pretend not to know you in public?
YES/NO/SOMETIMES

If you answered mostly yes or sometimes. This friend may not be the right person for you. Be open to having a heart to heart. You should never keep someone around who makes you feel bad about yourself.

Toxic Friendships

Find the strength to end the friendship. It's for your own good. Remember what I said about the sweater? Too much fixing, go shop around. I gave my friend too many chances. I was worried I wouldn't have another friend. I was **manipulated** to think no one would ever want to be my friend. So I lived in a toxic friendship much, much longer than I should have. The effects are damaging. Get out now! You have to stay strong and you cannot give into the peer pressure. Find the strength, to put the poison down. You deserve better and owe yourself fair treatment and to be around kind and loving people... I wish I learned that sooner.

Cleanse

Throughout my year, I spent a lot of my time on social media. Posting pictures, and blurbs about my day. In earlier chapters, I mentioned how things got mean and unbearable. I took a social media cleanse. I was no longer fixated on how many likes my pictures got or how many followers/friends I had. It's a great feeling.

Take the cleanse

This is the safest cleanse out there! You don't have to drink anything disgusting or shit yourself! Remove all social media apps from your phone.

We live in a world where we are validated by how many virtual friends we have. Take a step back and realize what is important to you. Go back online when you are feeling more stable and happy. Give yourself some time to breathe. Drop your phone, stop pressing the emoticons. You will be surprised by how much you like it.

Chapter 9: What Bullying Taught Me

There is so much that I learned while being bullied. I learned so much about self- love and empathy. I now understand that it's not me! That is something I never thought I would be saying in my life!

First, it may not seem like it, but you have choices; choices on how you let things affect you. Each day you have a choice to let people tear you down or there is the choice to let things go and end the cycle.

I know the words hurt, trust me,
I do, but there is no need to react
negatively. Carry yourself with confidence
and poise. Show them you are not a victim.
Come out stronger and don't let it get to
you.

It is more than okay to express your
feelings. Crying is okay, it can help
relieve some pain that has been bottled
up. Crying doesn't make you weak, it
makes you human. You are
acknowledging your pain and that is so
courageous.

Asking for help isn't easy, but it
is well worth it in the end!

There is a big difference between being
alone and being lonely. You may be lonely,
but you're never going to be alone. There
is always at least one person who has your
back. You may not know it, but they're
out there. I'm one of them.

I learned that it's not my fault. There is always going to be someone who doesn't like you. The people who have the problems with you are the people who have the problems.

People aren't always going to accept you and it doesn't matter what you do... Some people will always be narrow minded and choose not to like you. *Their loss*

Being bullied doesn't define you. It does define those who bully you.

There are going to be people who want you to change. They want you to change for them because it will be easiest for them. I learned you can't change for people. If they do not like you as you are, they are not worth keeping around, even if they are your best friends.

You can't get down on yourself for things you can't control.

Dropping the negativity in your life is such an amazing feeling. It's amazing what you can do when you are finally free. I have done more than I thought humanly possible during the year from hell. This was a year that tested my strength, my patience, my emotional, mental and physical capacity. I am proud to say I survived. I am amazed to say that I could have thrived in an environment that told me I couldn't. I found the positive and light in such a dark and sad time.

I know that deep down inside if I can do it, I am positive that you can do it too. All it takes is time, confidence, and the mind-set that IT GETS BETTER!

Chapter 10: Picking up The Pieces

As I mentioned in earlier chapters, I am in recovery. I have to figure out how to pick up the pieces and become the best me. I let the bullying dictate how my life was going to be. Physically, there was a lot of damage. My hair started coming out in clumps. I gained a significant amount of weight. I lost my mojo and became a person I am not very happy with. I asked myself every day for months:

"How do you turn this around?" To be completely honest, I am still figuring it out. I lost a large part of my identity. My best friend was such an influential piece of me. We were known together as a pair. Then we have leadership, this would have been my third year in the program. I am a little lost without it. I am going to be a senior. This is my swan song. I am beginning a new path for myself. An unknown path. I am learning each day about myself. I am taking charge of my health. I am not happy in my body right now. I let my emotional eating get the best of me. I am going to change. My hair is growing back in the sparse spots. My mental health is something I will always struggle with. I am happy today but I could be sad tomorrow. I let myself get so depressed, now I KNOW I can take charge of it. I am doing better though. I am stronger than ever; though I have days where I want to be alone... Alone time isn't bad. Everything is good in moderation. I have had more than enough time to reflect. The hardest part for me... Putting myself back out there.

Making new friends is terrifying. However, it is something that must be done so I can fully heal. The sad part about all of this is that no matter what or who I become friends with and all of the pain I went through, this girl will always have a special place in my heart... After all, she was my best friend. I do not want to remember all of the pain... but I think it is part of growing and it helps me grow and remember not to befriend anyone like that ever again.

You cannot control who hurts you, but you do have control on whether or not it hurts you. You can let the abuse take over your life, just like I did.

It's hard not to be sad and heartbroken over fleeting friendships. You have a chance to turn the page and start a new day. You're not going to get the reputation back that was destroyed... You have the option to start from the beginning and build up a new one. You will always have your character.

You are going to earn something better for yourself and create something beautiful. Pop that giant pimple you called a friend.
Turn the other cheek. Let yourself heal.
Truly, time is such an important factor. If you don't let yourself deal with your emotions, you will never recover or heal. This is the year for picking up the pieces. This is the year for me not to be the victim... This is the year to be Victorious! ♥

To the Educators, Parents, and adults of the world

Bullying affects more and more people each day. I beg you to take this issue seriously. There is no excuse for someone in your home, classroom, or on your team to be bullied or to be bullying someone else. It is not just kids being kids. Middle school and high school is such a hard time for many kids. Please give them your love, and support in this troubling time.

To the
Bystander

Step in. Help those who can't handle it on their own. Find the courage and be brave. Your actions can break the cycle!

To the bullied
and the bullies

Middle school and high school end. You are not going to be labeled like you were in school like you are going to be in the real world. People don't care. Are you going to bully after high school?

Cut the crap! We are all on the journey to self-acceptance. We just want to be liked by our peers. Bullies, please know what you're doing causes so much damage. I am sorry if you hurt yourself, but please find the courage to get some help. No matter what you are going through there is no reason to put someone else down to feel good. High school isn't the best four years of your life. There are so many opportunities for you after. Find the strength in yourself and be yourself. Don't conform to what people want you to be. Wear that wild outfit. Kiss your boyfriend or girlfriend. Be who you are inside. People are just going to have to accept it.

Focus on you, that's what matters in the big picture. Try new things and stay true to you!

Xoxo,

Madeleine

Take a Vow!

Being strong, confident and victorious is great, can you take a vow for yourself and commit? These are much more important than your wedding vows.

I promise to treat others and myself kindly. I vow to stick up for others and myself. I will live fully and authentically. I will accept others and myself for what makes me unique. I refuse to let others be without a voice. I will not hate myself. I will spoil others and myself with kind words. I will inform an adult I trust if I or someone else is a target of bullying. I promise I will not let the bullies run my life. I will make sure I will be myself. I promise that I will go from victim to victorious!

WAY TO GO!

It means so much to me that you decided to pick up my book. I have been working on this for a couple years now. I was going to write in the perspective of a bystander... however, plans change. I know firsthand it feels like things aren't going to change, and that you are going to continue to get hurt and feel bad. Good things are just around the corner for you. I found my path and my place and you will too. It just takes patience. I want to help get you through the hard times. As I said earlier, I wish I had this book last year. I would have done a lot better. I guess everything happens for a reason though. You are a strong person and you are going to get through this. You are not alone in this fight. There are so many people just like you and me. I am rooting for you!

You are not a victim. You are victorious

Resources and Advice

There are plenty of resources and tips out there to help those with depression as well as bullying. Friends and Family look for the subtle differences in appearance or mood.

I want you to know that there is no shame in getting help. It can only make you stronger. I didn't get professional help... I was embarrassed that I let my feelings get out of line so far that I felt this upset every day.

"It's just an expression"

Sadness and depression can really take over your face... literally. If you think a friend of yours is depressed look at their eyes.

Eyes are very expressive and the extra baggage can be especially evident on your face.

Not a care in the world in this picture. All I see is happy, happy, happy!

Again I look
very happy ☺

In this picture
there are a few
things different.
My eyes look worn
out, I am smiling.
But it looks forced.
My skin is also
looking extremely
stressed.

Here I am back in April on my birthday. I am well rested. I had a great day, but my eyes are just off. I look happy, but a scared kind of happy.

Here my eyes
look very tired,
I just look a
little glossy.
Stuck in a haze.

Here I am back to my old self. I am well
rested, my eyes are not stunned and this
is a genuine smile.

The point of that was to show that depression is something that not only is a chemical imbalance in the brain, but it can deteriorate you physically. In many pictures this year I look weak and on the verge of tears. These subtle differences in your expressions show a lot. If you notice any differences in a friend or family member, ask them how they are feeling.

You may find out more than you want to know, but it is a step in the right direction.

Cyber Bullying

We live in the world of the internet; this can be both a negative and a positive thing. The negative obviously being the concept of cyber-bullying.

If you are cyber-bullied…

Screen shot the message, the picture, the comment, etc.

Tell someone you trust,

Report the account on the corresponding social media website

I have had my fair share of cyber bullying. From late elementary school to present... Yes, I mean as in like 12 hours ago. I know what it's like to see the hurtful messages on the computer, on my phone, and on social media sites. People love to hate! Below are the best screenshots of cyberbullying and my ever so classy responses in the form of captions! Enjoy!

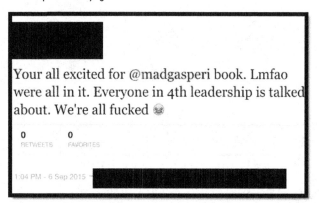

Your all excited for @madgasperi book. Lmfao were all in it. Everyone in 4th leadership is talked about. We're all fucked

0   0
RETWEETS   FAVORITES

1:04 PM - 6 Sep 2015

How embarrassing that you tweet an author with the wrong your (Laughing so hard I cry emoticon) Watch your language! Clearly some assumptions are being made. I never said anything about my book having anything to do with leadership. If you're so worried about being mentioned, you should have done the right thing.

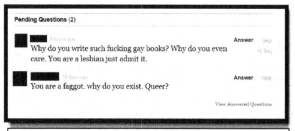

Pending Questions (2)

Why do you write such fucking gay books? Why do you even care. You are a lesbian just admit it.   Answer   Skip

You are a faggot. why do you exist. Queer?   Answer   Skip

View Answered Questions

I have the best answer for this one. I've said a million times Gay IS NOT an insult. I care because we are all human... I guess I exist to challenge ignorance and destroy homophobia

Shes hella fake...

Hella Fake Huh? Did you ever try speaking to me or getting to know me. Why am I fake? Is it because I am nice to everyone even when they are terrible to me? That's called maturity! If you took 5 minutes to get to know me you would have learned I am a passionate and caring girl who is just trying to find her place just like you! Next time if you're going to take a picture, tell me. I love a camera! I am very photogenic, though you didn't get my good side. Next time get to know me... we could have been great friends! I thought you were funny and we would have gotten along really well!

My Favorite Resources

You are never alone. There is always someone to help. Sometimes it is someone outside of your social circle. Below are resources for everyone. Whether you're LGBT+, a girl, a boy, or something in between. And you are dealing with depression or bullying... There is someone out there to help you.

http://theinspiringproject.com/

http://www.itgetsbetter.org/

http://www.glsen.org/

http://www.stopbullying.gov/what-is-bullying/

Trevor Lifeline - A crisis intervention and suicide prevention phone service available 24/7 at 1-866-488-7386

FREETrevorChat - A free, confidential, secure instant messaging support service

TrevorText - A free, confidential text messaging service

TrevorSpace - An online community for LGBTQ young people and their friends

Trevor Support Center - Where LGBTQ youth and allies can find answers to FAQs and explore resources related to sexual orientation, gender identity and more

Crisis Call Center

    800-273-8255 FREE or text
ANSWER to 839863

Twenty-four hours a day, seven days
a week
http://crisiscallcenter.org/crisisserv
ices.html
Depression and Bipolar Support

800-273-TALK FREE (8255) Twenty-
Four hours a day, seven days a week
http://www.dbsalliance.org

National Hopeline Network

800-SUICIDE FREE (784-2433)

800-442-HOPE FREE (4673) Twenty-
Four hours a day, seven days a week
http://www.hopeline.com
Crisis Center and Hotlines Locator by
State http://www.suicidepreventionlifeline.
org/getinvolved/locator

Suicide Prevention Services
Depression Hotline

630-482-9696

Twenty-four hours a day, seven days a week

http://www.spsamerica.org

Thursday's Child National Youth Advocacy Hotline

800-USA-KIDS FREE (800-872-5437 FREE)
Twenty-four hours a day, seven days a week
http://www.thursdayschild.org
Your Life Iowa: Bullying Support and Suicide Prevention

(855) 581-8111 FREE (24/7) or text TALK to 85511 (4-8 PM everyday)
Chat is available Mondays-Thursdays from 7:30 PM-12:00 AM

http://www.yourlifeiowa.org

Crisis Call Center
800-273-8255 FREE or text ANSWER to 839863
Twenty-four hours a day, seven days a week
http://crisiscallcenter.org/crisisservices.html

Depression and Bipolar Support

  800-273-TALK FREE (8255)
National Hopeline Network

  800-SUICIDE FREE (784-2433)

  800-442-HOPE FREE (4673) Twenty-
Four hours a day, seven days a week
http://www.hopeline.com

Crisis Center and Hotlines Locator by
State http://www.suicidepreventionlifeline.
org/getinvolved/locator

  Twenty-four hours a day, seven days
a week
http://www.dbsalliance.org

!Attention!

There is so much help out there for you! Please take it. Whatever you may be struggling with, there is someone who wants to talk to you and make things better. You just have to be open to getting help.

There is so much help out there for you! Please take it. Whatever you may be struggling with, there is someone who wants to talk to you and make things better. You just have to be open to getting help.

I am not a doctor, but if you think, medical treatment would be best for you. I advise you to seek the help. Talk to a parent. Teachers, a guidance counselor, a friend's parent, your next-door neighbor, your 2ND cousin twice removed.... It does not matter who you talk to, as long as you get the help you need.

The numbers and websites are here for a reason. Call, text. Your health is too precious to ignore!

Suicide

Suicide is never the answer. If you are ever feeling suicidal, please seek help. I have never been suicidal... but I have been depressed. I have felt depressed before, but I never got to that point. Please know that there are so many care about you... including me. Suicide is permanent, bullying is temporary. You have a whole life ahead of you. You are worthy of love, dignity, and respect. Suicide ends all of your chances of things getting better. Stay strong, be kind, and keep fighting the good fight! ♥

XO,

Madeleine

About Madeleine

Madeleine is an advocate, activist, author, and a student. Madeleine Gasperi is 17 years old. She debuted her writing by publishing a children's book entitled "I Have Two Dads: Different Types of Families."

In regards to writing, Madeleine has had goals of being published since she was a little girl. Madeleine is a huge advocate and ally of the LGBTQ community she believes in equality for all and overall creating a world where we are understanding and accepting of one another. Madeleine is a self-proclaimed kindness enthusiast.

Check out Madeleine's Other Books!

Madeleine's Links

Twitter:

@madgasperi

Instagram:

Madeleine_Gasperi

Join the social movement of kindness and keep in the loop on future projects and more!

I would just like to
thank everyone from
the bottom of my heart!
Thank you for the endless
support and praise. A big
thank you to everyone
who helped me when I
thought I was helpless.
Thank you for your
friendship.
I am extremely proud of
this book and I hope you
enjoyed it!

♥ You are Free!

Maddeleine Gasperi

If you've read this far,
use the '#'
#FromVictimToVictorious
or #MadeleineBook
to share your pictures, and
bullying stories! I'll be
checking! ☺
When you come across a
hashtag in the book, send it
to me! It's like virtual
book club!